Our PORTLAND

TEXT BY M. J. CODY
PHOTOGRAPHY BY RICK SCHAFER

Voyageur Press

This edition published in 2003 by Voyageur Press, an imprint of MBI Publishing Company, Galtier Plaza, Suite 200, 380 Jackson Street, St. Paul, MN 55101 USA

The information in this book is true and complete to the best of our knowledge. All recommendations are made without any guarantee on the part of the author or Publisher, who also disclaim any liability incurred in connection with the use of this data or specific details.

We recognize, further, that some words, model names, and designations mentioned herein are the property of the trademark holder. We use them for identification purposes only. This is not an official publication.

MBI Publishing Company titles are also available at discounts in bulk quantity for industrial or sales-promotional use. For details write to Special Sales Manager at MBI Publishing Company, Galtier Plaza, Suite 200, 380 Jackson Street, St. Paul, MN 55101 USA.

Library of Congress Cataloging-in-Publication Data

Cody, M. J. (Mary Jane), 1946-
  Our Portland / text by M.J. Cody ; photography by Rick Schafer.
     p. cm.
  ISBN-13: 978-0-89658-553-9
  ISBN-10: 0-89658-553-0 (hardcover)
  1. Portland (Or.)—Guidebooks. I. Schafer, Rick. II. Title.
  F884.P83 C63 2003
  979.5'49—dc21
                                                    2002152716

Edited by Kari Cornell
Designed by Maria Friedrich

Printed in China

Page 1: *Sacagawea, a Shoshone woman, guided the Lewis and Clark Expedition from the Ohio River Valley to the Pacific from 1805 to 1806. This statue, found in Washington Park, is of Sacagawea with her baby, Jean Baptiste.*

Page 2: *Downtown Portland and the Willamette River shimmer in the radiance of sunrise.*

Page 3: *One of Portland's historic cast-iron lampposts contrasts with the decorative façade of a modern building.*

Page 6: *The ornate colonnade of Old Town's New Market Theater, built in 1872, frames the 1983 U.S. Bancorp tower on a winter's evening.*

Page 7: *Even in the rain, flower vendors sell colorful bouquets on downtown street corners.*

Author's Dedication

To Mike Houck, for his endurance, passion, and commitment to keeping Portland green.

Photographer's Dedication

To my parents, Doris and Richard, who chose this beautiful city in which to raise our family.

Acknowledgments

Thank you to my late Grandmother and Grandfather Hafenbrack for sharing the city they loved, and to my parents who took us there to see ball games, ballet, symphony, and art. Thanks, too, to Susan, Goody, and Michelle for my beautiful homes away from home. And thanks to the diligent contributors of *Wild in the City*.—M.J. Cody

CONTENTS

WELCOME TO RIVER CITY

I grew up on the Clackamas River in Estacada, a small logging town thirty miles from Portland, a last stop on the highway before entering the wilderness of the Mt. Hood National Forest.

My grandparents lived in Portland and we visited often. The City—it was a magical place, where we fed ducks in manicured parks and ponds. Although they could have been the same ducks that landed on the river in front of our house in Estacada, in this setting they seemed like different creatures altogether.

I loved going downtown with my grandmother on the Hawthorne bus. This was a routine trip for her because she did not drive, but an adventure for me, riding with strangers high above the cars. We would go to the tearoom at Meier & Frank—Portland's marvelous department store—walk through the lovely parks, or visit the divine Multnomah County Library. There were so many amazing things to see in the city: Mannequins! Escalators! Statues and water fountains on street corners!

Over time I became smitten with the South Park Blocks. The elms and maples, so groomed and perfect compared to the untamed forest I roamed at home, offered summer shade and autumn spectacle. My grandparents were longtime members of the Portland Garden Club and the Portland Rose Society, so we often made our way to Washington Park to stroll through the acres of roses, stopping to smell nearly every one. High in the West Hills above downtown, the gardens frame a perfect view of Mt. Hood. That particular view and the exquisite fragrance of roses always remind me of my grandparents and their infectious exuberance for their Portland.

Going to Portland in those days—in the late 1950s and early 1960s—meant dressing for town. My mother would wear her nylon stockings, knit suit, and her alligator shoes with matching alligator bag on trips into Portland, where we'd attend a concert or shop for my ballet slippers in a tiny upstairs warren that was Nordstrom's. Yes, *that* Nordstrom.

One summer when I was twelve or thirteen, my mother bargained with my father that, if we were to spend several weeks fishing and clamming on the coast as we did every year, she wanted to spend at least one of those weeks in Portland

Above: *An accordion player entertains at the Portland Saturday Market in Old Town.*

Facing page: *The Hawthorne Bridge is one of five historic bridges spanning the Willamette River to downtown Portland.*

at a hotel. Mother was convincing, and she, my younger sister, and I stayed at the Roosevelt Hotel (now condominiums) on the sixth or seventh floor right downtown. The cacophony and bustle of the city at night was exhilarating and exotic to me. I can't remember sleeping at all. The nights seemed hotter than at home, and I would sit at the window in my nightgown and gaze at the lights, luxuriating in the warmth that radiated off the buildings as though I were absorbing a secret life.

My sister was not nearly as taken with the city's romance and sophistication as I was. When coastal rains brought my brother, his buddy, and my father to our hotel one evening, my sister and the boys shot suction cup arrows onto the door of our room. I confess, I joined in too, but when someone knocked on the door and said, "Quiet!" She giggled and wanted to keep playing. I was mortified.

The interesting thing about Portland is that it offers something for both that rambunctious sister who had little regard for decorum and the girl who yearned for a place with a touch of grown-up glamour.

Portland and glamour are not exactly synonymous, but for a kid from a small logging town, it was swell—just large enough to offer big city pleasures without being scary.

And that, I think, is why Portland is now landing on "best places to live" and "most livable cities" lists everywhere. We are friendly, receptive people in a welcoming, walkable city. We have terrific public art and transportation, great food, theater, and music. Comfortable and without pretension, Portland is a place where all can be themselves. Best of all, this relaxed city with an exceptional connection to nature still offers the luxuries of big-city life.

You can take a hike through Forest Park, which at 5,000 acres is the largest urban forest in North America, and spend the evening listening to jazz on the waterfront.

You can ski Mt. Hood in the morning, visit museums or the zoo in the afternoon, and still have time to dine in a world-class restaurant.

Major league basketball is within dribbling distance of Powell's City of Books, the largest, and possibly the best, bookstore in the world.

You can secure your kayak, canoe, or boat at RiverPlace Marina and walk to the movies or to a theater performance.

You can spend the entire day meandering on 160 miles of interconnected trails and greenspaces, enjoying any number of brewpubs along the way. (Portland has more microbreweries per capita than any other American city.)

You can visit Mill Ends Park, the teeniest park in the world (twenty-four inches square), and dance the night away on one of the last remaining "floating" dance floors at the Crystal Ballroom.

The "best places" citings are right on target. However,

keeping a city livable and in the forefront of urban planning the world over does not happen without a tremendous amount of effort. Portland is blessed with impassioned activists and planners who continually scramble to keep and improve what makes our city unique.

Thriving neighborhoods, including adjacent Old Town and Chinatown, surround Portland's vital downtown. The Pearl, Portland's newest upscale urban art district, is full of trendy, sophisticated shops and restaurants. Another lively neighborhood with intriguing boutiques, eateries, and historic homes is known simply as "Northwest," although recently the area has been referred to as "Nob Hill." The busiest streets in Northwest, accessible via trolley from downtown, are NW Twenty-third and NW Twenty-first.

The Sellwood District in southeast Portland is known for its antique shops and exceptional neighborhood cafés. Other interesting places to visit include the eclectic bohemian Hawthorne District, located directly east of downtown across the Hawthorne Bridge; NE Broadway near the Lloyd Center Mall; and the Alberta Neighborhood in North Portland. As neighborhoods grow and begin to define themselves, Portland just keeps getting better and better.

Over the years, Portland has become more of an old friend to me than that thrilling place of childhood. Despite this, the city still sometimes gives me that child's rush of delight. It is the same unadulterated feeling that my two-year-old niece expressed as we entered a taxi in New York and started down Fifth Avenue. Unprompted, she squealed and clapped her hands. That's it! That feeling of absolute joy for all the things that may be discovered in the city.

In *Our Portland,* I invite you to enjoy this special place we call home. You may not clap your hands and squeal with delight, but I guarantee this city will make you smile. Just a hint though: You might want to leave those suction cup arrows at home!

Water, Water, Everywhere—It's the Nature of the Place
A great blue heron cruises the waterfront. Beavers gnaw at an alder tree. An osprey executes a screaming dive into the river to spear a fish. A hiker slips on a slug. It's life as usual in the Pacific Northwest. Yet one thing is different—this is the city.

For those who live here, it's not unusual to share a par three, seventh hole with a heron rookery, or to see a stockbroker land a salmon from his boat on the way to work. In Portland, nature is not merely close at hand, but fundamental to the city.

Portland sits at the confluence of two great rivers, the Willamette and the Columbia, and although fully urbanized, we are influenced by nature. Salmon and steelhead still course through the heart of a metro area of 1.9 million people. Mt. Hood and the Cascade Mountain Range

Charming, refurbished vintage trolleys connect downtown to the Northwest and Pearl districts. Modern MAX (Portland's electric transit system) trains run from the airport and outlying districts to downtown.

provide backdrops to the cityscape. The great Columbia Gorge is less than an hour's drive, and the spectacular coast is only an hour and a half away. Portland's vast expanse of trails links parks and natural greenspaces, making us one of the "greenest" cities in the world. And Portland is the only city in the country with a volcano within its limits.

A History Etched in Stone

Our diverse landscape derived from a long and varied geologic history, including ocean and river sedimentation, volcanic eruptions, river erosion, and floods of astonishing proportions.

Tens of millions of years ago, western Oregon was part of a shallow sea. At the same time in the east, the volcanic Cascade Range was forming. Uplift drained the sea, and the massive lava flows from volcanic eruptions covered the Portland area with several hundred feet of Columbia River basalt. The volcanic basalt remains under much of the Portland metropolitan area; in many places in and around Portland, especially in the cliffs of Oregon City and the Columbia River Gorge, the basalt is clearly visible.

But the most recent series of cataclysmic events sculpting our landscape occurred during the last Ice Age: the floods. Some 12,000–15,000 years ago, glacial ice dammed the Clark Fork River in western Montana, causing tremendous volumes of water to accumulate (estimated to be about half the volume of Lake Michigan). When the ice dam broke, it sent a colossal flood across eastern Washington, down the Columbia River Gorge, and into the Willamette Valley. There may have been as many as forty of these catastrophic floods, referred to as the Missoula or Bretz floods, as the ice dam re-formed and failed many times. It is estimated that floodwaters reached an elevation of about 400 feet above sea level in the Portland area, depositing huge amounts of silt, sand, and gravel, and sculpting much of the hill-and-gulley landscape (such as Sullivan's Gulch where I-84 sits) characteristic of Portland today.

And Then There's the Rain . . .

Portland is known for its rainfall, but we really only average about thirty-six inches annually (less than Atlanta, Houston, Baltimore, Indianapolis, and Seattle). When it does rain in Portland, it does so in small amounts over a long period of time, as opposed to short, heavy downfalls. For the nine months between November and July, drizzle, mist, sprinkles, or showers keep the city green. "Showers" means it is not raining constantly, even though it may seem as if it is. Because the weather is not harsh and there are "sunbreaks" interspersed with those showers, most Portlanders participate in outdoor activities year-round. We have a mild climate (winters in the low 40s; summers in the high 70s)

The windows of downtown Portland reflect a stunning sunrise.

and very seldom have snow in the city. In winter we are weather watchful. We wait for winter storm warnings, which do not keep everyone hunkered down at home, but have many of us heading out for nearby mountains and snow, or to the ocean shores and headlands to watch tremendous waves.

Even though Portland is wetter than most places, it is not an umbrella town. Perhaps it is that stubborn pioneer spirit that makes opening an umbrella seem like a weakness. Besides, what are parkas and hooded raincoats for? And why do you need the nuisance of an umbrella when one of those sun-breaks could occur at any moment?

Stump Town, Recent History

Before the Lewis and Clark Expedition of 1805–1806 and the great pioneer migration of 1843–1880, the Portland area was inhabited by self-sustaining indigenous peoples who valued and respected the tremendous bounty of the nearby rivers and forests.

A few curious sea captains and trappers who traded with England's Hudson Bay Company knew of the Willamette River. But Lewis and Clark passed it by twice in 1806 before exploring what the Indians referred to as Multnomah, a river that was barely visible behind wooded islands, marsh, and thickets. The Willamette gets its name from the Indian term *Wallampth,* or "green river," the name the native inhabitants used to refer to the water above the falls at Oregon City. Multnomah, which means "down the river," was that portion of the river below the falls.

The arrival of the pioneers meant paradise found for the thousands who ventured across the Oregon Trail or arrived by ship, but it meant paradise lost to the indigenous. Wave after wave of immigrants made land claims of 640 acres each. The few natives who survived the "white man's" diseases such as small pox were supplanted.

Oregon City was first platted by Hudson Bay Company's Dr. John McLoughlin in 1829. Situated near Willamette Falls, which provided plenty of salmon for eating and water power to operate lumber and grist mills, the tiny town became the center of activity and enterprise. In 1843, however, William Overton and Asa Lovejoy ventured in search of a deepwater port and a more expansive site than Oregon City, which was hindered by its steep basalt cliffs. Twenty miles down river they found what they were looking for and laid claim to present-day Portland. Soon tired of the massive task of clearing the heavily timbered site, Overton drifted on, and an Oregon City entrepreneur, Francis Pettygrove, bought his share of the claim. The new partners, Lovejoy and Pettygrove, were unable to agree on what to call their newly platted clearing and decided to toss a coin—Boston, for Lovejoy from Massachusetts; or Portland, for Pettygrove from Maine. Pettygrove won.

By the late 1800s, Portland was a boom town that had surpassed Oregon City's population and industry. But Portland was not the kind of place Lovejoy and Pettygrove envisioned. The mill and port town attracted a seamier side of life. Houses of ill repute and saloons flourished. A new trade of "shanghaiing"—kidnapping young men and selling them to ship captains—was in full swing. Joseph "Bunco" Kelly was one of the most notorious racketeers and kidnappers. Many bar owners and hotel operators relied on the shanghai trade to earn extra cash. In one attempt to make a quick buck, Kelly delivered a wooden dime-store Indian wrapped in blankets to a ship. When the captain learned the next morning that his new crew member was a wooden statue, he threw it overboard. Men operating a dredge nearly sixty years later claimed to have recovered the statue.

Near the turn of the twentieth century, money from the lumber business and the California Gold Rush infused the seedy port town and expanded export trade, causing downtown business districts to sprout and prosper.

Simon Benson, a teetotalling lumber baron and philanthropist, personified the swing from the hell-raising, raucous town to a more civilized place. Benson, concerned with his workers' drinking habits, commissioned twenty bronze freshwater drinking fountains to be installed around town. There is an account (some say by Benson himself) that saloon business decreased 25 percent after the fountains were in place. Sixty "Benson Bubblers" are currently located throughout the city. (Ironically, Portland is now renowned for its microbreweries.)

New wealth changed the temperament and the face of the city. Before long, buildings of architectural merit, parks, theaters, public art, and mansions graced the up-and-coming city. Portland had grown up. It has been reported, though, that Portland retained some of its rustic beginnings as late at the 1920s—old growth stumps still marked a few intersections.

Welcome to Oregon, Now Go Home

Oregonians tend to be an independent and eccentric lot. Many families, descended from the hardy stock of pioneers, loggers, trappers, and seafaring folk, arrived in the area generations ago, seeking the "promised land." We may at times be obstinate, but Oregonians are generally gracious, welcoming, and exceedingly friendly. We are a people willing to "live and let live."

Oregonians, too, have long been known for having a conscience. Land use policies, mandated public beaches, and environmental laws were established in Oregon long before other states considered such things. Oregonians considered the land-grabbing frenzy of the 1980s, however, certain doom to the "real" Oregon way of life.

The neighborly openness once so innate here began to shift to hostility towards the thousands of Californians who swooped in and gobbled up real estate. As early as 1973, Governor Tom McCall lobbied that Oregon "must be protected from grasping wastrels of the land." He believed firmly that "unregulated growth leads inexorably to a lowered quality of life." Some joked that Tom McCall's motto for Oregon should be: "Welcome to Oregon, now go home."

Those days are tempered, but many Oregonians—old-timers as well as the newly established—are cognizant of the unusual loyalty to place and amusingly advise others: If you used to live somewhere else, just don't admit it publicly.

Even though growth is of eminent concern, the uproar over new settlers from the south was somewhat erroneous. Oregon is a land of immigrants. Portland prospered in the real estate boom. Perhaps the most recent influx was just a modern version of the California Gold Rush.

The positive changes that newcomers bring to the city are undeniable. Portland has enthusiastically embraced the rich heritage of the Pacific Rim, as well other cultures. Restaurants, the arts, public transportation, and architecture are revitalized. Portland is no longer the frontier town it once was. Today's challenge is to retain Portland's distinct character. Portlanders tend to be democratic and diverse, original, quirky, and independent, yet they share common sensibilities. An amusing list of identifiers sums up what it means to be a Portlander.

Kids and adults alike love feeding the ducks at Crystal Springs Rhododendron Garden. In winter, nearly 100 species of waterfowl can be found here.

You are a Portlander if:
• You throw an aluminum can in the trash and feel guilty.
• In the winter, you go to work in the dark, come home in the dark, and only have a six-hour day.
• The bride is registered at Columbia Sportswear Company.
• You consider that if it doesn't have snow on it or has not recently erupted, regardless of elevation, it is a "hill" and not a "mountain."

• You are sitting at a downtown red light. The light turns green and the car in front of you does not move. You do not honk. After another light change, you approach the driver to ask if they need any assistance.
• You find a wallet with $500 and give it back to the owner.
• You know more people who own boats than air conditioners.
• You know more than ten words for rain.
• Every day is casual Friday.

Those who are newly arrived and those who have been here forever agree that Portland is an exceptional city. Let Rick Schafer's excellent photography take you on a tour of the city, then come see it for yourself. Welcome to Portland, *Really.*

Chronological History of Portland and Oregon

1579: *Sir Francis Drake believed to have visited Oregon.*

1778: *Captain James Cook lands at Cape Foulweather and reports on wealth of fur on the Northwest Coast.*

1792: *Captain Robert Gray enters the Columbia River and names it after his sailing ship, the Columbia.*

1803: *Louisiana Purchase extends United States to Rocky Mountains.*

1805–1806: *Lewis and Clark Expedition explores lower Snake and Columbia Rivers and establishes Fort Clatsop, near Astoria.*

1818: *United States and Great Britain agree to "joint occupancy" of Oregon.*

1825: *Dr. John McLoughlin, Chief Factor for England's Hudson Bay Company, builds Fort Vancouver across the Columbia from what would become Portland.*

1829: *Dr. John McLoughlin establishes a claim at Willamette Falls, later named Oregon City.*

1830: *Fever pandemics begin calamitous death toll of Indians.*

1843: *First large migration of U.S. emigrants arrives via Oregon Trail. Francis Pettygrove and William Overton claim land that will become Portland.*

1846: *Sam Barlow and Philip Foster open the Barlow Road, the most significant "last leg" of the Oregon Trail. First newspaper,* Oregon Spectator, *founded in Oregon City.*

1848–1860s: *During the California Gold Rush, Portland becomes wealthy from exports.*

1850: *The* Oregonian *newspaper is established in Portland.*

1859: *Congress grants Oregon statehood on February 14.*

1903: *John Charles Olmsted plots Portland parks and greenways.*

1948: *Vanport Flood destroys low-lying area of Portland in hours.*

1962: *Columbus Day Storm causes major damage.*

1970s: *Landmark conservation bills, including the Bottle Bill, which banned aerosol sprays, approved. Land Conservation Development Commission created.*

1980: *Mt. St. Helens erupts, disrupting ship traffic on Columbia River.*

1980s: *John Charles Olmsted's 1903 Master Parks Plan, including a "40-mile loop" linking parks and greenways is realized. (Expanded now to 160 interconnected miles.)*

Morning mist begins to dissipate with sunrise at Ecola State Park on the Oregon Coast. Haystack Rock and the small coastal town of Cannon Beach are visible in the distance.

THE CITY OF PERPETUAL CURIOSITY

I am in the Tower of Cosmic Reflections, sipping tea from a small ceramic bowl. A lid covers the bowl, and, if I tip the cup just right, the tea leaves will not land on my lips as I drink. Gripping the lid and bowl with both hands, I sip. I try to reflect serenely on the cosmos but am really only concentrating on not dumping the hot tea in my lap. The woman sitting across the table from me simply sips then pulls the leaves from her upper lip and smiles at me as she places them carefully on a small saucer.

The woman and I are strangers but we end up strolling through the Classical Chinese Garden together. She is seventy-nine and has come to experience a part of the city she has not yet discovered.

We behold structures with names such as Reflections in Clear Ripples, Flowers Bathing in Spring Rain, and Knowing the Fish Pavilion, where, unfortunately, we neither see, nor get to know any fish.

I exit through the Hall of Brocade Clouds and proceed down the street to MAX, Portland's light rail system, which suddenly seems woefully named. I take MAX to PGE (Portland General Electric) Park where I meet my friend Mike, and we settle in to eat hot dogs, drink beer, and watch Portland Beavers baseball. As we watch the game on an exquisite summer's eve, the stadium becomes our own Tower of Cosmic Reflections, and we start to dream up new names for civic attractions and for the city itself.

The list of nicknames for Portland—River City, Rose City, Stump Town, Rip City (as the Blazers basketball announcer calls it)—does not seem to encompass the true spirit of the city. Yes, Portland does have the finest collection of movable bridges in the world and plenty of roses. Portland once had lots of stumps, and the Blazers can rip, yet somehow . . .

Hey, how about The City of Perpetual Curiosity?

Above: *Thirsty anyone? In a strategic move to keep his lumber mill workers sober, Simon Benson made certain there were freshwater fountains for everyone. The bronze "Benson Bubblers" can be found throughout downtown.*

Facing page: *Historic Union Station, built in 1893, brightens Portland at twilight. In the station's heyday, ninety-two trains called on Portland daily. Service has dwindled to less than half that amount, but Amtrak's Coast Starlight, the Empire Builder, and the new Cascades service from Eugene to Vancouver B.C. still make scheduled stops at the station.*

Above: *The Interstate Bank tower rises high above the delicate flowering trees of springtime.*

Right: *Sunrise captures the city and RiverPlace Marina in a moment of grace.*

Above: *As dawn breaks, all is quiet at Waterfront Park.*

Right: *On a rainy day in Portland, these men countenance the rain, while the women take refuge under umbrellas.*

Facing page: *The steel trusses of the Broadway Bridge frame the skyline of downtown Portland.*

Downtown Portland is an intriguing mélange of architectural styles.

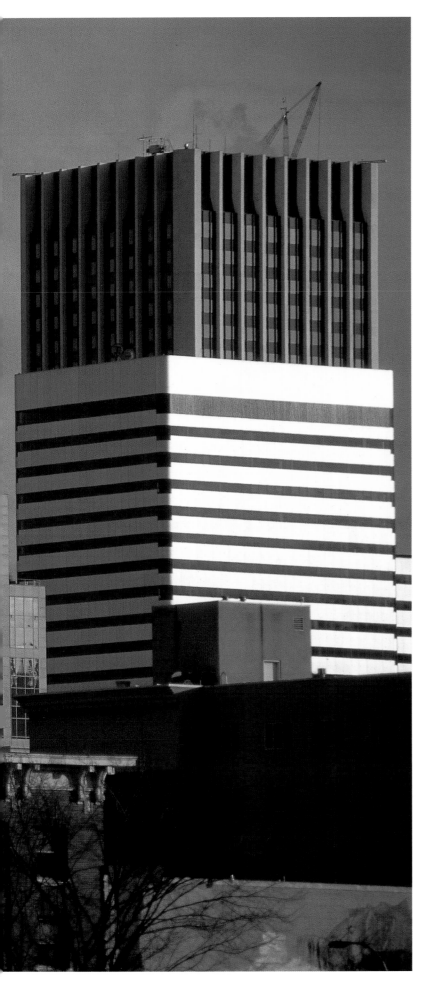

Early 1900s lampposts are preserved throughout the city.

Above: *The Portland Brewing Company's Brewhouse in northwest Portland is one of twenty-eight microbrewery sites in the city.*

Right: *Portlanders love their beer. The newly expanded interior of the Portland Brewhouse taproom and grill provides a bright and cheerful setting in which to indulge in a handcrafted a brew.*

Facing page: *Standing sentinel at daybreak, a majestic Douglas fir Christmas tree graces Pioneer Courthouse Square. Seasonal festivities in the square include Christmas concerts performed by choral groups from schools around the state.*

Above: *The Fremont Bridge, Portland's newest, carries those traveling on Interstate 405 across the Willamette River.*

Right: *Canada geese, our year-round guests from the north, paddle in the Willamette.*

Facing page: *The Hawthorne Bridge, finished in 1910, is the oldest surviving vertical lift bridge in the world. The counterweights (seen on the towers) each weigh 450 tons.*

Rhododendrons in bloom accentuate the Ira C. Keller Memorial Fountain. The top level emulates brooks running through a tree-shaded plaza before cascading over "cliffs" to form waterfalls.

An ornamental pot of tulips brightens downtown Portland.

The waterfront marina at RiverPlace is within walking distance of downtown. Leisure boating and water skiing are popular pastimes on both the Willamette and the Columbia. "River City" is not a misnomer.

Dusk is a perfect time for reflection. These people pause on the harborside walkway at Tom McCall Waterfront Park.

The stone sculpture garden is one of many public art installations along Tom McCall Waterfront Park. Across the Willamette River, the twin spires of Portland's Convention Center can be seen through the cherry blossoms.

Above: *Busy U.S. Highway 26 intersects Portland as it traverses the 450 miles from the Oregon coast to the Idaho border.*

Left: *A touch of green ivy enhances this old brick building in downtown Portland.*

The 1912 Steel Bridge is one of the only known dual-lift bridges in the world. Here, the lower deck accommodating Amtrak and freight trains is lifted for one of Portland's many pleasure crafts. Lift operators are on duty twenty-four hours a day. In the summer, Portland bridges open nearly 300 times a month.

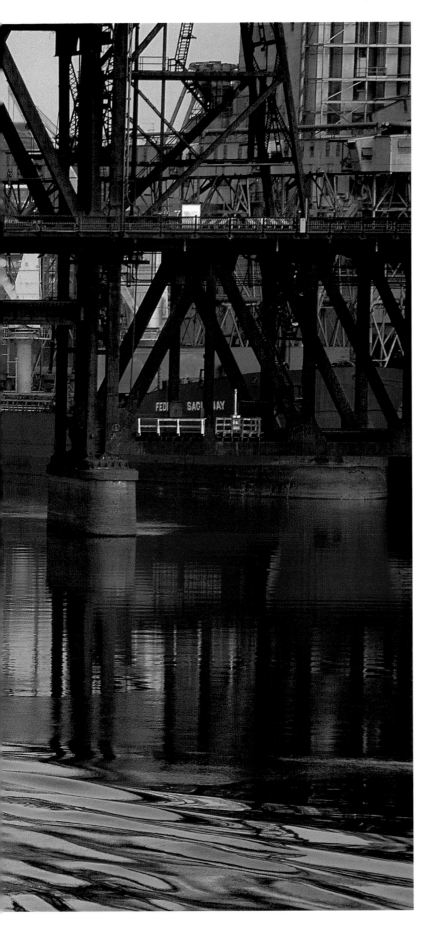

A cargo crane on the commercial ship Ocean Wave *unloads on the Willamette River.*

Behind this ship docked on the Willamette River downtown stand the Broadway and the Fremont Bridges.

Above: *Oaks Bottom was Portland's first wildlife refuge. A premier hiking destination, the untamed, backwater wilderness located within the city is home to more than 100 species of birds.*

Right: *David P. Thompson, Portland's mayor from 1879–1882, presented the city with the Plaza Fountain at Fourth Street Park as a watering trough for horses. This bronze elk sculpture, which sits atop the fountain's base, always reminds me of my grandfather, who loved it.*

Facing page: *The Salmon Street Fountain in Governor Tom McCall Waterfront Park spouts one of its many formations at sunrise. Mt. Hood looms in the background.*

September and October, months with little rainfall, are generally the best time of year in Portland. Autumn leaves in Governor Tom McCall Waterfront Park offer a dazzling display.

Pink cherry blossoms reflect in a pond on the Nike Campus in Beaverton, a Portland suburb. Nike, of "Just do it" fame, started in Portland thirty years ago. The NikeTown store downtown on SW Sixth Avenue is entertainment in itself.

Portland's staid city hall, built in 1895 and renovated in 1998, contrasts with its modern neighbor, Michael Grave's famous Portland Building.

A Long Way From
T-I-M-BRRRR!

*I*n 1850 Charles and Sarah Talbot established a homestead in the heavily forested West Hills above downtown Portland. They began clearing a wilderness rife with black-tailed deer, Roosevelt elk, timber wolves, black bear, and cougar. Their daughter, Ella, dashed down the hill to school on her pony accompanied by the family dog.

That Portland is remote from what it is today, but the vigorous rough-hewn history of the city and its proximity to nature infuses us.

Portland's founders were vigilant about incorporating art and parks into the city plan. Old Town's Skidmore Fountain, Portland's first piece of public art built in 1888, started a tradition. Today, one percent of all capital building budgets is set aside for public art.

Many of Portland's public art projects depict a connection to the wild. Bronze river otters, bear, salmon, and deer are only a few creatures that can be found near Pioneer Courthouse Square, the central downtown plaza. Abstract animals and plants are also used to identify bus kiosks. In Old Town Portland's Chinatown, Portland's sister city, Suzhou, contributed to the creation of The Classical Chinese Garden, the largest authentic Ming dynasty urban garden of its kind outside of China. In this serene setting, nature and the built environment find balance.

Portland's thriving arts community includes dance and ballet, professional theater companies and smaller art houses, and a distinguished variety of music ranging from symphony and chamber music to blues and jazz.

Art galleries flourish throughout the city. On the first Thursday of each month, city streets come alive when galleries and shops open late for public viewing. The Portland Art Museum recently added a new Center for Native American Art, featuring exquisite masks, totems, and artifacts of Northwest and national indigenous peoples.

Portland's American Advertising Museum, created in 1886 by the local advertising, marketing, and media community, is the only one of its kind in the United States. The museum displays award-winning television commercials and advertising pieces, including the famous Burma Shave roadside placards.

Although little girls no longer ride ponies to school fearful of cougar, wolves, or bear, don't be surprised if you see red tail hawks soaring between high-rise buildings and peregrine falcons nesting on bridges. Portland is a city that exists with nature, not in spite of it.

Above: *The weathered hands of a street performer strum lightly, adding ambiance to the Portland Saturday Market.*

Facing page: *Stone lions guard the ornate ceremonial Chinatown Gate in Old Town Portland, protecting and welcoming all who enter.*

Stones representing mountains stand tall along the "lake" in the Garden of Awakening Orchids—Portland's Classical Chinese Garden. The five cardinal elements of a typical classical Chinese garden are all present in the photograph: stone, water, architecture, plants and poetry (in the form of calligraphic inscriptions).

A flowering oleander contrasts with the ornately carved wooden doors of a pavilion in Portland's Classical Chinese Garden.

This striking silhouetted statue of a pioneer mother stands above the cloud cover at Council Crest Park in Portland's West Hills.

VALIANT MEN HAVE THRUST OUR FRONTIERS TO THE SETTING

This pioneer family, weary horse, and covered wagon represent the thousands who undertook the migration to the Oregon Territory from 1843 to 1900. The marble carving stands outside Oregon's Capitol building in Salem.

The Pittock Mansion was once the private home of Henry Louis Pittock, founder of the Oregonian *newspaper. The mansion sits 1,000 feet above sea level and commands a view of five mountains in the Cascade Range—Mounts St. Helens, Adams, Rainier, Hood, and Jefferson.*

Top left: *Japanese cherry trees blossom and daffodils bloom in the Pittock Mansion gardens.*

Top right: *Pansy and rhododendron blossoms are left as offerings at this decorative stone wall mosaic in The Grotto.*

Left: *The Grotto, officially named the National Sanctuary of Our Sorrowful Mother, is a sixty-two-acre Catholic shrine and botanical garden. The Portland landmark offers tranquility to all denominations.*

Facing page: *The sculpture courtyard adjacent to the Portland Art Museum is a welcome resting and lunching site for many.*

From the inside of OMSI, Oregon Museum of Science and Industry, there's a great view of the Willamette River. Although it is not visible in this photograph, the museum keeps a submarine on display in the river.

A young girl plays among the banners in the wind exhibit at the Oregon Science Museum and Industry.

Facing page: *One of the windows is real in this eight-story mural painted on the Oregon History Center. The center's museum is the repository for Oregon's historical artifacts and features ongoing exhibits, a library, archives, and a wonderful gift store.*

Neon sign of the old Portland Theater stands out against the night sky. The theater is now the Arlene Schnitzer Concert Hall.

Informal dress-rehearsal concerts beckon summer theatergoers at the Arlene Schnitzer Concert Hall, known as the "Schnitz."

Left: *These unique crystal light fixtures, designed by the McMenamin brothers and Hippo Hardware, adorn rooms throughout the historic Crystal Ballroom facility, a favorite place to go dancing during the 1920s and 1930s. Ballbearings suspend the ballroom's floor, making it "float." In 1997, the brothers saved the structure from demolition.*

Below: *The Heathman Hotel doormen, clad in "Beefeater" costumes, are easy to spot.*

The Portland Saturday Market sign provides a folksy contrast to the streamlined U.S. Bancorp tower.

A candlemaker, one of many local artisans, displays his wares at the Saturday Market.

Above: *A happy vendor at the Portland Saturday Market reads the paper while attending his booth of wooden games and toys.*

Left: *Street musicians are a lively addition to the weekly Saturday Market—an informal venue for good fun, arts, crafts, and local produce.*

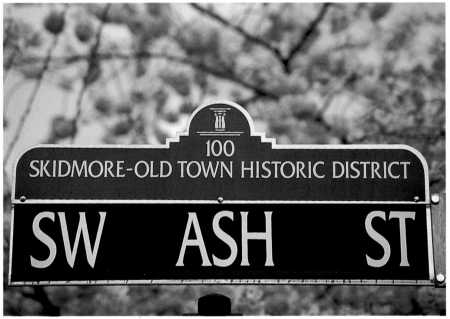

Above: *The "Made in Oregon" sign sits above the outlet store for Oregon goods and delicacies at the west end of the Broadway Bridge downtown. The famous sign originally advertised White Stag skiwear, established in 1929.*

Left: *This street sign stands out against the profusion of cherry blossoms in downtown's Skidmore–Old Town Historic District.*

Facing page: *The U.S. Bancorp tower rises above the historic New Market Village and Skidmore Fountain in Old Town Portland. The Skidmore Fountain was Portland's first piece of public art.*

A peacock struts its stuff at the Oregon Zoo.

Portland is renowned for its readers, and it's not unusual to find several relaxing in the South Park Blocks. Powell's City of Books, just a few blocks away, is one of the largest bookstores in the world.

Above: *Children sit on bronze sculptures as they watch colorful butterflies in the zoo's Butterfly Garden.*

Left: *Portland is not known for its butterflies, being too cool and damp to support many of the spectacular creatures, but this lovely specimen and others can be found at the zoo.*

GREAT BLUE HERONS AND ROSES

The Portland Rose Festival is the city's premier civic event. I still associate the celebration with a minor disaster of childhood. The day before the Grand Floral Parade, my father, who was not handy with tools, built a "garage" (read: roof held up by posts). After watching the parade in town, we returned home to find the structure collapsed. Rather than hearing cursing or ranting, I only remember laughter.

Rose Festival activities consume nearly the entire month of June, the time when our gorgeous roses are at their peak. Governor Tom McCall Waterfront Park on the banks of the Willamette becomes a focal point of excitement with the arrival of the naval fleet and the ongoing carnival. The city hums with air shows, the colorful Dragon Boat Races, museum exhibits, dance and music performances, and the prestigious three-day Portland Arts Festival, which features artists from all over the world who display their wares in the beautiful South Park Blocks.

Other Portland events throughout the year include the Mexican fiesta Cinco de Mayo; Homowo, a vibrant festival of African arts; the outstanding Waterfront Blues Festival; Portland Bite, a celebration of our fabulous local restaurants; Oregon Brewers Festival; Portland International Film Festival; and the annual Portland Creative Conference, which provides an opportunity for Hollywood and advertising leaders to share ideas. The creative conference is the brainstorm of claymation animator Will Vinton, of M&Ms and California Raisins commercial fame, whose studio is in town.

The great blue heron is Portland's official city bird. The famous bird is featured on the label for BridgePort Brewing Company's Blue Heron Ale and on the heron Weather Machine (a weather-predicting kinetic sculpture). And Portland wouldn't be Portland without Blue Heron Week, a celebration of the bird, which features food, music, biking and hiking tours, and guided canoe trips to nearby Ross Island to view the heron rookeries.

So settle back, turn the page, and join in our celebrations.

Above: *The brilliant lights of the Rose Festival carnival bring the city to life. The annual event draws thousands for fun, games, food, music, and breathtaking rides on the waterfront.*

Facing page: *Fireworks light up the sky over the Willamette River during Portland's Fourth of July celebration. The Hawthorne Bridge is illuminated for the festivities.*

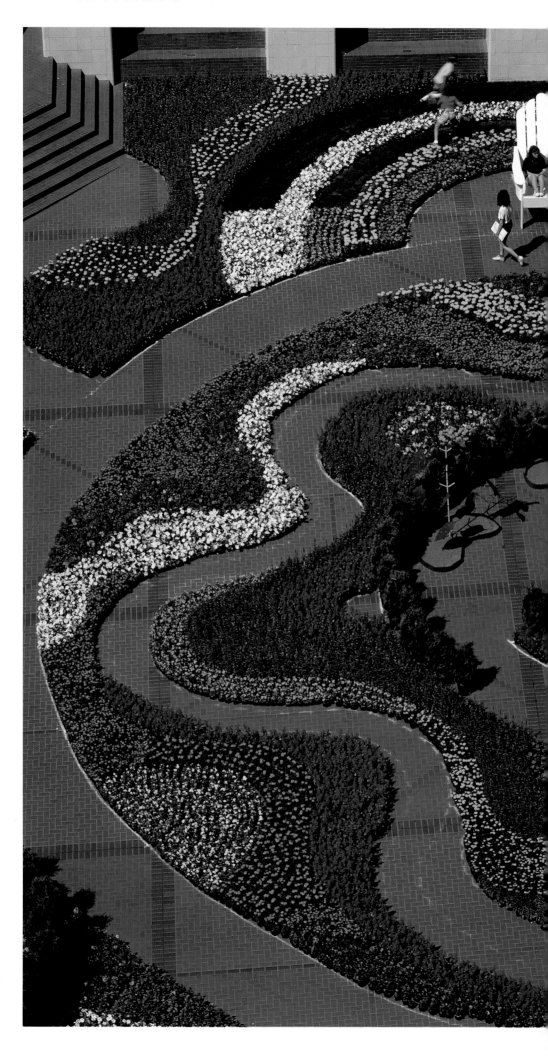

Each year during the Rose Festival the delightful Festival of Flowers maze decorates Pioneer Square.

A tug assists a Naval fleet ship to anchor as the U.S. Coast Guard stands by.

The tail of a Navy helicopter sits in the foreground of Rose Festival preparations on the waterfront. The U.S. Bancorp building, stunning against the blue sky in the background, looks as though it is a painted backdrop.

Dragon boats are moored at the RiverPlace Marina downtown. The Rose Festival dragon boat races on the Willamette feature crews from various groups and corporations around the world. Local crews practice on the river all year round regardless of rain, sleet, or snow.

Riding clubs from all over the state participate in the Rose Festival's Grand Floral Parade.

A happy participant shows off her prize ribbon in the Grand Floral Parade float competition.

Grand Floral Parade floats typically have an amazing amount of detail.

The annual summer Waterfront Blues Festival draws vast crowds onto the lawns near the RiverPlace Marina and RiverPlace Hotel. Many blues lovers listen to the music from their boats.

A guitar riff punctuates a set at the Waterfront Blues Festival.

Musicians take a break at the blues festival.

Above: *A meticulous builder pays attention to details on his sand castle tower.*

Right: *Competitors construct sand sculptures at the annual Sand Castle Festival at Cannon Beach on the Oregon Coast. Haystack Rock can be seen in the background.*

FROM THE MOUNTAINS, TO THE PRAIRIES, TO THE OCEAN . . .

*O*regon dazzles in its scenic splendor. The volcanic Cascade Range runs through the center of the state, separating the dramatic plateaus and the arid wheat and sagebrush plains of the east from the lush green forests and valleys of the west. The spectacular Columbia River Gorge defines the Oregon-Washington border. The Snake River and Hell's Canyon, the deepest gorge on the continent, divides our eastern border from Idaho. To the west, sandy beaches and magnificent headlands extend 400 miles down the coastline.

There's nothing like driving this diverse state. When I was a kid, we'd often get up on a rainy Saturday morning and decide to take a trip east of Mt. Hood to my Uncle Bill's logging camp. There was never an argument about these spontaneous departures. We all knew it meant sun. I still love to astonish visitors from out of state with a drive starting in Portland in the rain and ending at The Dalles, Bend, Sun River, or Kah-Nee-Tah in the sun.

In Oregon, it is entirely possible to frolic in the mountains and play at the beach on the same day. Day trips out of Portland can fit many a mood. Meander through rural farmland of the Willamette Valley, stopping to taste wine in one of the region's wineries. Take a drive along the Mt. Hood loop, which includes the Columbia Gorge, Hood River orchards, and Timberline Lodge. Take a leisurely train trip to Eugene and Lane County's covered bridges. Explore the beaches. Hike, river raft, fish, swim, or simply immerse yourself in a wonderland of forests, rivers, and lakes. A little farther afield is our shining gem Crater Lake, famous for its intense cobalt blue. At 1,932 feet deep, it is the deepest lake in North America.

From the impressive high deserts and cowboy country to the splendid shores of the Pacific, welcome to our wonderland.

Above: *A fly-fisherman casts at sunset. Sport fishing is a common pastime on Oregon's bountiful lakes, streams, and rivers.*

Facing page: *Along the spectacular Columbia River Gorge, which divides Oregon from Washington, the Vista House sits atop Crown Point. The Historic Columbia River Highway, finished in 1922, provides access to the house. The narrow, curving highway winds along the steep cliffs of the gorge, offering close-up views of marvelous waterfalls. A seventeen-mile stretch from Troutdale to Multnomah Falls has the largest concentration of high waterfalls in North America.*

Douglas firs of Mt. Hood National Forest are dusted in snow. At the foot of Mt. Hood is a typical logging clear-cut.

Above: *Many of the runs at popular SkiBowl offer impressive views of Mt. Hood.*

Right: *Historic Timberline Lodge was constructed in 1937 as one of President Roosevelt's WPA projects. Utilizing mammoth timbers, native stone, and imaginative ironwork, the lodge itself is a showcase of the work of local artisans and craftsmen.*

Clouds and fog hide the Willamette Valley as the sun rises behind Mt. Hood.

From the Mountains, to the Prairies, to the Ocean . . .

Oregonians and visitors alike love beach-combing our sandy ocean shores. Oregon has 400 miles of magnificent coastline to explore.

Facing page: *A wind-swept pine withstands the weather at Ecola State Park on the Oregon Coast. In the distance, Haystack Rock stands against the headlands.*

Above: *Hot air balloons inflating in a vineyard appear to be gigantic exotic produce growing among the grapes.*

Right: *Howard Hughes's famous* Spruce Goose HK-1 Hercules *is on exhibit at the Captain Michael King Smith Evergreen Aviation Educational Institute in McMinnville. The enormous plywood flying boat diminishes the other historic planes.*

Facing page: *A hot-air balloon floats over the verdant spring vineyards of western Oregon. There are 168 wineries in the state, many less than an hour's drive from downtown Portland.*

This view of the Columbia River and Mt. Hood under a full moon illustrates why the Columbia Slough is a popular site for houseboats and boaters.

A rhododendron in bloom embellishes Dr. John McLoughlin's house, a national historic site in Oregon City. Known by the indigenous peoples as "The Great White Eagle," and designated the "Father of Oregon," Dr. McLoughlin headed Northwest outposts for Britain's Hudson Bay Company. He platted and settled Oregon City in 1929.

Fishermen ply the waters below the Willamette Falls at Oregon City. The annual spring and fall Chinook migrations up river are widely anticipated. Portland General Electric's turbine power plant is on the right, a paper mill is on the left.

A fisherman at Trillium Lake appears completely at ease amid the stupendous scenery of Mt. Hood and Mt. Hood National Forest.

LIVING NATURALLY

I am sitting at a downtown café with my friend Georgia, talking about the publicity Portland has gotten lately in national magazines. Georgia points out that the articles are filled with clichés. Portlanders are avid coffee drinkers. Portlanders are unparalleled readers. Portlanders are so attuned to the environment that they eat organic food, wear hiking boots everywhere, and hop on mountain bikes at every opportunity.

We are amused by this since we know the city to be dynamic and filled with all sorts of people, yet, as we glance out the window, an athletic, gray-haired man sits at an outdoor table sipping coffee and reading a novel. He is wearing hiking boots. His mountain bike leans against the building. As though that weren't enough, as we leave, a young man in shorts—and, yes, hiking boots—passes us carrying an oar. A book is tucked under the other arm. We laugh. Clichés are clichés because they are true. But don't mistake Portlanders for yokels. Many wear those hiking boots and carry those books to some very stylish cafés!

Above: *A father and young daughter enjoy a profusion of daffodils, the sure sign that spring has sprung.*

Facing page: *A majestic Ponderosa pine reaches for the sky. The lush forests of cedar and Douglas fir give way to pine trees and sparse undergrowth east of the Cascade Mountain Range.*

Portland is tagged as a casual, outdoorsy town. And it is that. With rivers and an abundance of greenspaces, we are never far from nature. But the main thing about Portland is its ability to embrace all types. We are comfortable in our own skin. Meet me for a brew at the Lucky Lab or martinis at Bluehour.

As for the coffee? Yes, Portlanders are coffee fiends rivaled only by microbrew devotees. We also have an unprecedented number of excellent restaurants specializing in local bounty such as clams, salmon, shrimp, oysters, berries, nuts, and farm produce.

The readers? Yep, they're everywhere. There's an old joke about why so many settlers who traveled the Oregon Trail lost their way and drifted to California: those who came to Oregon were able to read the sign.

So I invite you to relax and enjoy this most livable of cities. And don't worry, no one will point and laugh if you're not wearing hiking boots.

The limb of an oak tree stretches toward the rhododendrons and azaleas in Laurelhurst Park, one of Portland's oldest parks established in 1909. Glorious pink "snow" from cherry blossoms covers the ground.

Above: *Autumn leaves sprinkle the granite stairs on the pathway to the Japanese Garden in Washington Park.*

Left: *In this captivating view of Laurelhurst Park's natural spring-fed pond, mature fir, maple, and willow trees are reflected on the surface of the water. At one time, a white swan named General Pershing patrolled the pond, attacking anyone who approached the water's edge.*

At this exquisite moment, the Moon Bridge in the Japanese Garden looks as though it's the entrance to an enchanted forest.

Bright patches of spring welcome visitors at the Washington Park entrance. Washington Park, Portland's premier park, is home to the Zoo, the Rose Gardens and amphitheater, Hoyt Arboretum, the World Forestry Center Museum, the Japanese Garden, and the Wildwood Trail.

Tennis and roses go together well in Washington Park.

Above: *Young blooms are a sweet counterpoint to Washington Park's old, moss-laden stone wall.*

Right: *Washington Park offers spectacular views from the amphitheater and International Rose Test Garden. With more than 8,000 varieties, the garden is famous worldwide.*

Above: *A carved narrative on the black granite walls of the Vietnam Veterans Living Memorial in Washington Park chronicles both the experiences in Vietnam and the events on the home front.*

Right: *A couple enjoys a sunny afternoon on the steps at Terry Shrunk Park.*

Facing page: *Gorgeous forest trails wind through Tryon Creek State Park, the only state park in the nation within a major metropolitan area. The park is famous for its trillium festival in early spring.*

Above: *The 185 interactive water jets of the Salmon Street Fountain divert kids (and adults) on hot summer days.*

Left: *Bikers await the starting signal for the annual Providence Bridge Pedal.*

Facing page: *A lone tree is silhouetted dramatically against a reflected sunset over Mt. Hood.*

Sailboats cruise downtown near Ross Island, home to a large heron colony and an eagle nest.

Portland's only suspension bridge, the 1931 St. John's Bridge, arches beautifully across the Willamette River. Located a few miles west of downtown, it connects North Portland to U.S. Highway 30.

A crew team rows past houseboats near Ross Island and Oaks Bottom National Wildlife Refuge on the Willamette River.

Above: *A father and child enjoy a rare snowfall*

Left: *Snow blankets the 175-acre Hoyt Arboretum, which includes more than 900 different species of trees and shrubs. The Dawn Redwood, a species thought to have been long extinct until a few specimens were discovered in a remote area of China, also grows here.*

A gray sky reflects somberly in the Washington Park reservoir.

WHERE TO GO FOR MORE INFORMATION

POVA (PORTLAND OREGON VISITORS ASSOCIATION)
Pioneer Square
715 SW Morrison
Portland, OR 97205
(503) 275-8355 / (877) 678-5263
Events Hotline:
(503) 525-3738
www.pova.org
or www.travelportland.com

Oregon Tourism Commission
775 Summer Street NE
Salem, OR 97301-1282
(503) 986-0000 / (800) 547-7842
www.traveloregon.com

Resource Books
Best Places Portland, 5th edition, Kim Carlson, Sasquatch Books, 2001.

Portland Bridge Book, 2001 Revised Edition—a history and guide to Portland's bridges. Sharon Wood Wortman, Oregon Historical Society Press.

One City's Wilderness: Portland's Forest Park—history and maps. Marcy C. Houle, Oregon Historical Society Press, 2000.

Wild in the City—a Guide to Portland's Natural Areas—a comprehensive guide to parks, greenspaces, hiking, biking, boating, natural history in the Portland metro area. Eds. Mike Houck & M. J.Cody, Oregon Historical Society Press, 2000.

Facing page: *Visitors to Pittock Mansion can look across Portland shipyards to flat-topped Mt. St. Helens. A volcanic eruption on May 18, 1980, removed the top 3,000 feet of the mountain and downed more than 4 billion board feet of usable timber.*

ABOUT THE AUTHOR AND PHOTOGRAPHER

*M*J. Cody is the editor of *Best Places to Stay: Pacific Northwest*, and co-editor with Mike Houck of *Wild in the City*, a guide to the Portland metropolitan area greenspaces. An Oregon native, she spent many years in L.A. where she was the photo editor of the *L.A. Weekly* and an award-winning art director for *Flowers&,* a flower industry magazine. MJ also wrote for television series *Major Dad, Mama's Family,* and *Knots Landing.* She won the Soap Opera Award for "Best Storyline" two years in a row for her work on *Knots Landing.*

MJ writes a regular column called "Wingin' It," which appears in the Travel section of the Sunday *Oregonian.* She writes features for the *Oregonian,* the *Seattle Times, NW Palate Magazine,* and other publications. She currently is developing a television series on livable cities.

*R*ick Schafer has lived in Oregon all of his life. Rick's passion for photography began when he was a student in high school. His stepfather, the late Ray Atkeson, had a significant influence on Rick's photography and the development of his own creative photographic style. What began as a hobby has become a full-time profession. Rick's work, which showcases the state of Oregon, the Oregon coast, and Oregon's golf courses, has been internationally published in regional calendars and several coffee table books. In addition to traveling the Northwest to capture the beauty of the region, Rick manages his own extensive stock library and has recently branched out into commercial photography and digital services.